Pebble®

How Fruits and Vegetables

T0080595

Carrots Grow Underground

by Mari Schuh

Consulting Editor: Gail Saunders-Smith, PhD

Consultant: Sarah Pounders, education specialist
National Gardening Association

CAPSTONE PRESS
a capstone imprint

Pebble Books are published by Capstone Press,
1710 Roe Crest Drive, North Mankato, Minnesota 56003.
www.capstonepub.com

Copyright © 2011 by Capstone Press, a Capstone imprint.
All rights reserved.
No part of this publication may be reproduced in whole or in part, or stored in a retrieval system, or transmitted in any form or by any means, electronic, mechanical, photocopying, recording, or otherwise, without written permission of the publisher.
For information regarding permission, write to Capstone Press,
1710 Roe Crest Drive, North Mankato, Minnesota 56003.

Library of Congress Cataloging-in-Publication Data
Schuh, Mari C., 1975–
Carrots grow underground / by Mari Schuh.
p. cm.—(Pebble books. How fruits and vegetables grow)
Summary: "Simple text and photographs describe how carrots grow underground"—Provided by publisher.
Includes bibliographical references and index.
ISBN 978-1-4296-5280-3 (library binding)
ISBN 978-1-4296-6185-0 (paperback)
1. Carrots—Juvenile literature. I. Title. II. Series: Pebble (Mankato, Minn.). How fruits and vegetables grow.
SB351.C3S38 2011
635′.13—dc22 2010025471

Note to Parents and Teachers

The How Fruits and Vegetables Grow set supports national science standards related to life science. This book describes and illustrates how carrots grow. The images support early readers in understanding the text. The repetition of words and phrases helps early readers learn new words. This book also introduces early readers to subject-specific vocabulary words, which are defined in the Glossary section. Early readers may need assistance to read some words and to use the Table of Contents, Glossary, Read More, Internet Sites, and Index sections of the book.

Printed in the United States 5685

Table of Contents

Under the Soil 5
Growing 9
Flowers and Seeds 17
Many Vegetables Grow
Underground 19

Glossary 22
Read More 23
Internet Sites 23
Index 24

Under the Soil

Green stems and leaves sprout from the soil. Underground, vegetables grow larger and larger every day.

Life Cycle of a Carrot

Plant roots grow underground. People eat the roots of some plants. Carrots are one kind of root vegetable.

Growing

Carrots start as tiny seeds. They are planted in cool weather. In one to three weeks, seedlings slowly grow above the soil.

Under the soil, the carrots grow longer and thicker. Deep, loose soil helps carrots grow long and straight.

Long stems and lacy leaves
grow from the carrot tops.

After two to three months,
crunchy vegetables
are pulled from the ground.

Flowers and Seeds

Carrots that stay underground
all winter grow flowers
and seeds the next year.
Later, the tiny carrot seeds
become new carrot plants.

radishes
beets
parsnips

Many Vegetables Grow Underground

Many vegetables grow
the way carrots do.
Radishes, beets, and parsnips
are other root vegetables.

onions
potatoes

Onions and potatoes start their life in the ground too. Vegetables grown underground give us healthy food to eat.

Glossary

root—an underground plant part that takes in nutrients and water to be used by the plant to grow; some plants grow roots that store a lot of nutrients; people eat these roots as vegetables

seedling—a young plant that has grown from a seed

soil—earth in which plants grow

sprout—to start to grow

stem—the long main part of a plant from which leaves and flowers grow

Read More

Edwards, Nicola. *Vegetables.* See How Plants Grow. New York: PowerKids Press, 2008.

Spilsbury, Louise. *Vegetables.* Eat Smart. Chicago: Heinemann Library, 2009.

Tagliaferro, Linda. *The Life Cycle of a Carrot.* Plant Life Cycles. Mankato, Minn.: Capstone Press, 2007.

Internet Sites

FactHound offers a safe, fun way to find Internet sites related to this book. All of the sites on FactHound have been researched by our staff.

Here's all you do:

Visit *www.facthound.com*

Type in this code: 9781429652803

Index

beets, 19
flowers, 17
leaves, 5, 13
onions, 21
parsnips, 19
potatoes, 21
radishes, 19
roots, 7, 19
seedlings, 9
seeds, 9, 17
soil, 5, 9, 11
stems, 5, 13
winter, 17

Word Count: 152
Grade: 1
Early-Intervention Level: 21

Editorial Credits
Erika L. Shores, editor; Bobbie Nuytten, designer; Wanda Winch, media researcher; Laura Manthe, production specialist

Photo Credits
Bill McCarthy, 6 (bottom), 16; Capstone Press: Karon Dubke, 4, 6 (middle, top), 8 (all), 12, 14, 18 (middle), 20 (top); Getty Images: Johanna Parkin, 10; Shutterstock: Alexey Bragin, cover (soil), Christopher Elwell, 20 (bottom), chungking, (carrot design element), Irina Zolina, 18 (top), Jo Mikus, 18 (bottom), ultimathule, cover (carrots)

The author dedicates this book to her friend Gene Mayer, who refuses to eat vegetables such as carrots and desperately wants to believe beef is a vegetable.